Bra

Henry Slesar

Alpha Editions

This edition published in 2021

ISBN : 9789355890115

Design and Setting By
Alpha Editions
www.alphaedis.com
Email - info@alphaedis.com

BRAINCHILD
BY HENRY SLESAR

Ron Carver's day was beginning strangely.

For one thing, the legs he swung off the narrow bed wouldn't touch the floor. And his hands, whose ten strong fingers could manipulate the controls of any ship ever launched into space, were weak and clumsy.

He looked at the hands first, looked at them for a long time. Then he screamed.

He screamed until footsteps were loud in the corridor outside his room; shrill, piping screams that didn't stop even when the giant woman-face was bending over him, speaking gentle, soothing words, stroking his thin shoulders with giant, comforting gestures.

"There, there, now," the woman was saying. "You're all right, Ronnie. You're all right. It was only a nightmare... a bad old nightmare...."

She was right. Only the nightmare hadn't ended. The nightmare was before his face, in her gargantuan features, in her motherly touch on his frail body, in the sight of the small, soft appendages that were his hands.

They were the hands of a boy of twelve. And Ron Carver was thirty years old.

Two men giants joined the woman at his bedside, and one of them forced a small speckled capsule past his resisting lips. Then his viewpoint became detached and distant, and a pleasurable drowsiness overcame him. He stretched out and shut his eyes, but he could still hear the worried tones of their speech.

"Dr. Minton warned us," one of the men said, lifting Ron's bony wrist and feeling for the pulse. "The boy has suffered some severe traumatic shock..."

Dr. Minton! Ron Carver's mind grasped the familiar name—the name of his own physician—gratefully. But his body gave no sign.

"Maybe we better call him," the woman said nervously. "I think he's still in the sick bay."

"Good idea."

In another moment, a familiar hairy face was floating over Ron's head like a captive balloon, a face grown grotesque in size.

"Doctor..." he said with his lips.

"There." Dr. Minton patted his shoulder. "You're all right now, Ronnie. You're perfectly all right. Just relax and try to sleep." The balloon came closer, and the scraggly ends of the doctor's beard brushed his cheek. Then the doctor's mouth was covering his small ear.

"Play the game," the doctor whispered. "For your own sake. Play the game, Ron..."

Then he was asleep.

He awoke to the sound of running feet. He sat up in bed and looked towards the door of the small white room in which he was confined. It was partly open, and the sound of clattering soles and shrill young voices came through clearly.

The door slammed open, startling him. A hoydenish youngster gaped at him. There was a flat lock of reddish hair over his forehead, and his face was freckled.

"Hoy," he said. "What's the matter with *you*?"

Ron stared back wordlessly.

"You sick or something?" the boy said, edging into the room.

"No." His own voice, strange and reedy, frightened him. "No, I'm all right."

"Andy!" A tall man with a frowning face appeared behind the boy. "Come on, fella. Let's not waste any time." He looked at Ron. "You the new chap?"

"Yes."

"Feel well enough for some breakfast?"

"I guess so."

"Fine. Then get some clothes on and come along."

"Hoy," the freckle-faced boy said curiously. "You play airball?"

"That's enough of that." The man paddled the boy's rump. "Get along, Andy. You'll have plenty of time to get acquainted later."

The boy giggled and ran down the hall. Ron got out of bed slowly, and walked towards the undersized clothing that was draped on a nearby chair. He slipped into a gray coverall and said: "Listen—can I talk to you?"

The man looked at his watch. "Well ... all right, I suppose. But only for a minute. I promised the boys a game this morning; I'm Mr. Larkin, the athletic director."

Ron hesitated. "Mr. Larkin, I—where am I?"

"Don't you know?" Even the man's smile was half a frown. "You're at Roverwood Home for Boys. Didn't they tell you that?"

"No," Ron said carefully. "I—I don't seem to remember very much. How I got here, I mean."

"Dr. Minton brought you in last evening. He's one of our directors."

"Oh." Ron laced on the tiny scuffed shoes. "And where's Dr. Minton now?"

"Gone back to the city. He's a busy man. Hear they've got him working on some big government project. Well, come on, Ronnie. Breakfast's waiting."

"Yes, sir," Ron Carver said.

He followed the tall man down the hall, having trouble guiding the short stumpy legs that were now his own. They entered a communal dining room, filled with the clatter of dishes and the laughter of boys. He was brought to a long table and seated beside Larkin. The other boys greeted him with only mild interest, but the freckle-faced youth at the other end dropped him a broad wink.

He ate sparingly, choking on the food, his mind working. It was the longest nightmare of his life, and the moment of awakening seemed too far off for comfort.

Then Larkin was standing up and rattling a spoon against a water glass.

"Fellas," he said, "all those interested in this morning's airball game will assemble on the field in half an hour after breakfast. Please don't volunteer unless you're able to handle a PF. Everybody else is invited to see the game."

He sat down, amid cheers. He smiled sadly at Ron, and asked: "How about you, Ronnie? Can you operate a PF?"

"Of course," he answered, without thinking. He'd been using Personal Flyers since he was old enough to dream about flight. On his tenth birthday, his father had bought him one of the earliest models, a cumbersome machine then called a "platform". Since that day, he had become familiar with every man-made thing that flew, from the double-rotored PF's to the sixty-rocket space liners.

"Fine," Larkin said cheerfully. "Then maybe you'd like to play the game."

Ron Carver looked up sharply. *Play the game....*

"Sure, Mr. Larkin," he said, forcing his eagerness.

Half an hour later, they were assembled on the huge lawn outside of the main building of Roverwood Home for Boys. The long row of PF's, looking like chrome-plate pot-bellied stoves, gleamed in the morning sun. The boys began to run when they saw their Flyers, and Ron found his arm taken by the freckled youth who had entered his room.

"Hoy," he said. "Follow me. I'll pick you out a lively one!"

The redhead clambered inside a machine marked Seven, and Ronnie followed his instructions by choosing the vehicle marked Nine. They secured themselves inside, and tested the jet tube set in front of the Flyer. The boys took off from the ground in perfect unison, the redhead bellowing out an introduction over the sound of the wind roaring past their ears.

The PF's descended on a blast from Mr. Larkin's whistle, congregating in the center of the field. Teams were chosen, and Andy was picked as Captain of the Odds. A coin was tossed to decide the playing sequence, and they were ready.

Larkin released the first airball, and the two teams streamed up after it. Andy gunned the engine and reached the ball first. He sent it scooting thirty yards ahead of him with the blast of the airjet pipe, but a member of the Evens team was there to veer it off to the left. Another Evens man, a burly youth of fourteen, took command of it, neatly getting the airball in the sight of his airjet and cork-screwing it towards the goalpost. Ron had grown too old before the game of airball had become popular with the nation's youngsters, but he had seen enough action to have learned some tricks. He pointed his PF directly for the Even machine, and kept coming. The burly youth looked up, startled at the onslaught, and pulled his Flyer away. The fact that the PF's were magnetically collision-proof didn't matter; it was pure instinct. Ron captured the ball in his airjet pipe, and shouted for Andy to block his path towards the goal.

The Odds scored, and the two teams descended for a rest. Andy, the grin wide on his brown-spotted face, said: "You're okay, Ronnie! Hoy, I mean it. You're okay!"

"Thanks," Ron said. He found himself panting.

The game resumed. It ended in a 3-2 score, favor of the Odds. Andy and Ron were cheered as they left the Flyers and headed for the communal showers of the Roverwood Home for Boys.

In the stall, Ron Carver looked down at the spindly frame that was now his body, and began to weep. Andy heard him, but said nothing. Then they dressed and ambled back to the main house, sharing the awkward silence of new friends.

Finally, the older boy said: "I don't mean to butt in, Ronnie. But is somethin' the matter?"

"I—I don't know, Andy. I'm all mixed up. I don't even know how I got here."

"That's easy. Dr. Minton brought you."

"But where is he now, Andy? Dr. Minton? It's very important that I see him."

Andy shrugged. "Not much chance of that. Dr. Minton only comes around once, twice a year.

"But I have to see him! Right away! Will they call him for me?"

"Gosh. I don't think so. He's some kind of big shot in the government now."

They flopped on the grass, and Andy tore out a ragged clump and chewed on it blankly. Ron said: "Andy, I'm in trouble. I need some help."

"No kidding?"

"Yes!" He brought his voice to a whisper. "Andy—what if I told you that I was really—" He stopped, and examined the open, innocent face in front of his eyes. He knew that it would be useless to tell the truth. "Skip it," he said.

"I don't get you. What's on your mind, Ronnie?"

"Nothing, Andy. I just have to get away from here."

"But you can't. I mean, not until they let you. It's the rules."

"Andy—how long have you been here?"

The boy thought a moment. "Almost nine years," he said blissfully. "Since my folks got killed."

"How long do you have to stay?"

"Why, 'til I'm old enough to work. Eighteen, I guess."

Only six years to go, Ron thought sourly.

He stood up.

"Andy—where do they put the PF's?"

"In the shed."

"Is it possible to get one out?"

"'Course not. Only when we play the game."

"And when will we play another game?"

"Dunno. Tomorrow maybe. It's Sunday."

Play the game. Ron said to himself.

The Evens team member caught the spinning, gas-filled airball in the path of his airjet and kept it moving in front of his Flyer. Andy was after him in a flash, shouting for Ron to join him. But Ron's daring tactics of yesterday seemed to have deserted him. He steered the PF out of the path of the Evens man, and the goal was scored.

On the ground, Andy said: "What's the trouble, Ronnie? Didn't you hear me?"

"Yes, I heard you. Andy, listen. I'm taking off—"

"Sure, in just a minute," the freckled boy said. "But, look, the next time you see me cut across the—"

"You don't understand!" Ron said intensely. "I'm running away!"

"What?"

Larkin's whistle sounded the signal to resume play. The airball shot into the sky, and the two teams sped after it. Andy was late getting started. He looked at Ron and gasped: "You can't do that—"

But Ron Carver was already in flight, and his PF was heading away from the center of the action, heading over the jagged pinetree tops that surrounded the Roverwood Home for Boys, heading for the misty green hills beyond.

Larkin saw what was happening, and he blew his whistle shrilly. The teams descended, thinking a foul had been called. Larkin shouted a command towards the burly youth who had played so aggressively the day before, but then realized it was far too late to stop the swift passage of the PF now disappearing behind the trees.

Ron dropped the PF to earth as soon as his eyes spotted the first sign of a settled community. He landed the small machine in the shadow of a hillside, and dragged it into the thick underbrush for concealment. Then he trekked to the main highway, until he reached a road sign that informed him of his location. He was in a town called Spring Harbor, just fifteen miles outside of the city.

He looked down at the waxy newness of his gray Roverwood coverall, and wondered if it was a familiar uniform to the residents. But he had to take the chance. He covered the cloth with dust, and rolled up the trouser legs almost to his knees. Then he broke off a long branch from a sapling and used it as a walking stick. Casually, he strolled into the town proper.

The pose worked. Some people on the porches looked after him with mild curiosity, but no one stopped him. Then he paused at a gas station, and asked the owner of the automatic pump if there was transportation available to the city.

The owner scratched his face and looked at the boy curiously. Ron told a plausible story about being separated from a scouting group, and the man seemed satisfied. He had a pick-up copter going into the city at ten o'clock; he invited Ron to wait inside his house, and even served him a sandwich.

The copter pilot, a genial red-faced man, asked him some gentle questions. Ron answered them guardedly, and told him that his destination was Fordham Terrace. The copter dropped him on the rooftop of the massive office building, and the pilot left with a friendly wave of his hand.

When he was gone, Ron rolled down his trouser legs, brushed his uniform clean, and descended to the fourteenth floor of the building. He walked rapidly along the corridors until he came to the door marked:

WILFRED G. MINTON, M.D.

He rattled the knob. When he found the door locked, he let out an adult oath. It was Sunday, of course. Dr. Minton wouldn't be in on Sunday. And Ron had never known his home address.

He returned to the elevator and went to the ground floor. There was an information booth, and the woman behind the glass was a motherly type. Her eyes softened at his approach.

"Dr. Minton?" she said, lifting an eyebrow. "Why, I guess I do have his address. But who sent you, young man?"

"Nobody," Ron said. "I was supposed to see him, that's all."

She kept her eyes on his face while her hand leafed through the directory on her desk. "Of course, Dr. Minton doesn't use his office anymore. He gave up his practice here almost a year ago. He was put on an important government project. Dr. Jurgens, his assistant, handles all his patients now. Would you like Dr. Jurgens' number?"

"No," Ron said. "Please. I must see Dr. Minton."

"All right. But I don't know if you can see him without an appointment. He's staying at the Government Medical Center in Washington." She smiled. "That's a long way for a little boy...."

"Thank you," Ron said curtly, and walked off.

His mind was racing, tripping over his thoughts. A year ago! But that was impossible! It seemed only days since he had returned from Andromeda, after a five-year absence. One of his first visits had been to Dr. Minton's office—not just to renew an old friendship, but to allow the physician to examine him thoroughly for traces of the varied and deadly diseases that man was subject to on alien worlds. Could it have been a whole year ago? Where had he spent the time between? And what had happened to give him the body of a twelve-year-old child?

He fought off the questions. He had no time for the puzzle now; there weren't enough pieces to make sense. He had only one thought: to find the doctor.

But that was a major problem all by itself. Washington was a good hour away by fast copter service. And in this big, suspicious city, it wouldn't be as easy to obtain free transport to his destination. He could do nothing—not without money.

When he thought of money, he thought of Adrian.

Adrian....

Of course! Adrian would know what to do next. Adrian always seemed to know what to do. Her father's money had opened every conceivable door in this city, and she herself had often suggested that it open doors for him. Doors to the executive heights of the Space Transport Company. Doors to the plush offices in the sky tower, doors to the select circle of cigar-smoking men who controlled the transportation empire of which Ron had been only a spare part. But Ron Carver had been young (he thought now, sourly) and his head had been stuffed with ideals. He detested the groundworms who stayed home and counted the profits of space travel. He wanted the stars.

So he had become a pilot, one of the best in her father's fleet. She had sworn at him for his decision, and turned away from his embrace. But on the night of their parting, the night before the dawn ascent towards the speck of light that was Andromeda, she had softened, and cried in his arms.

He thought now of that moment, and his small fingers rolled into fists.

Adrian, he thought. *I must go to her....*

The doorman was magnificent and imposing in his braided uniform, but his eyes were cold when he saw Ron.

"What do you want, son?"

"I—I have a message for Miss Walder. It's very important."

"Okay, son. You just give your message to me."

"No! I'm supposed to deliver it in person!"

The doorman grunted. "Wait a minute." He put in a call to the penthouse apartment. The idea of a twelve-year-old visitor must have amused the girl. He brought back an invitation for Ron to enter her home.

Ron stepped off the elevator, and his stomach was churning. What would she say when she saw him? Would she believe his story? Would she help him find an answer?

Adrian came to the door herself, and the amusement was evident on her long, smoothly-planed face. Her auburn hair was swept back in Grecian ringlets, and the gown she wore was blindingly white. "Come in, dear," she said, smiling.

The effect of looking up at the girl, now a sort of giantess in his eyes, made Ron dizzy. He swayed against the doorframe, and her cool fingers steadied him.

"You poor boy," she crooned. "Come inside."

She half-carried him to the downy sofa. For a full minute, he was too choked to speak. She offered him a glass of milk, but he asked for water. She brought some to him, and he coughed.

"Now," the girl said, spreading the wide skirt over her knees, "just what was it you wanted to tell me?"

"I—"

"Come now." She smiled endearingly, and brushed back the hair from his forehead. "You must have had something on your mind."

"Yes," he said at last, his voice strained. "Yes, Adrian. I—I'm Ron...."

"What?"

"I'm Ron Carver! No, listen, I'm not mad. It's really me, Ron!"

She had stood up, shocked. Then she laughed.

"Adrian, listen to me! Something happened to me when I returned from Andromeda. I don't know what. I found myself at a boy's home near Spring Harbor."

"Now, really! This is the craziest—"

"I know it's crazy!" He wiped his forehead in an adult gesture. "But it's true, Adrian. I've been—changed somehow. I don't know why. But it's something to do with Dr. Minton."

She sat down again, limply. Then she studied his face, and for a moment, Ron thought she was seriously considering his predicament. But then the laugh started again, the same slightly off-key laugh Ron remembered.

"Adrian, you must believe me! I can prove it! Just listen to me for a moment!"

She stopped the laugh and grew serious, her eyes caught by the intensity of his own. "All right," she whispered. "I'll listen...."

"My name is Ronald Carver. I'm thirty years old. I'm a Captain of the Walder Space Transport Company. I have been in the Andromeda system for the past five years. I returned to Earth—" he stopped, and swallowed hard. "I don't know exactly when. I went to see Dr. Minton, an old friend and a physician. He examined me, and then—"

She stared, fascinated.

"And then I was a child! A child of twelve, in a home for boys. I ran away from there this morning, and came looking for Dr. Minton. I've been told that he's in Washington. I must get to him. I must find out what's happened to me—"

She was shaking her head, slowly, eyes still fixed on his face. He got up from the sofa and came towards her. His small hand reached out and patted the fine bones of hers.

"You must remember," he said. "You must believe me, Adrian. Remember our last night together? Right here? We stood by that window, and you cried in my arms. And then we...."

She tore her hand away, as if burned. Then she stood up, looking horrified.

"Get out of here!" she shrieked. "You little monster!"

"Adrian—" Only now did he realize what it must have been like to her, to hear those words from his childish lips, to feel the touch of his tiny hand as he spoke of the night they....

"Get out!" she cried, covering her face. "Get out before I call the police!"

"Adrian!"

She screamed, piercingly. This time, the sound brought heavy foot-side clumping outside her front door. It was thrown open, and a uniformed man with bouncing epaulets was striding towards him.

"No," Ron said. "You must listen—"

"Get him out of here!"

"Sure, Miss Walder!"

He struggled in the big man's grip, while the girl turned her head aside. He managed to squirm from his hold, and broke for the door. The houseman started after him, cursing. Ron's hand went out and grasped a solid metal ash tray. He threw it without thought or aim, but it crashed squarely into the man's face and sent him thudding to the carpet.

Adrian screamed again. He looked at her once more, imploringly. Then he ran for the door, just before she reached for the house telephone.

In the elevator cage, he punched the button marked roof, and fell against the wall, panting.

On the rooftop, he galloped across the metallic surface towards the ledge. He peered over it, and his heart sank when he saw that his stratagem had deceived no one. Police were entering the building, and some were pointing fingers in his direction. With a sigh, he dropped to his knees and rested his head against the cool aluminum surface.

"It's no use," he said aloud.

Then he heard the copter overhead.

He looked up, thinking it was a police vehicle. But then he saw the outmoded design of its fuselage, and the young face at the controls.

It hovered over his head, and a rope ladder unfolded. The youthful pilot said: "Quick! Climb in!"

He blinked at the voice, unbelievingly. Then he scrambled to his feet, and grabbed the dangling ladder. He barely made it into the copter; the pilot had to help.

"Who are you?" he said, gasping.

The boy laughed. "I hate cops, too."

Then they were in the air, and speeding towards the west.

Ron Carver watched the back of the young boy's neck for twenty minutes, while he steered the ancient copter expertly across the skies. He figured that the boy might have been fourteen or fifteen, but there was a competence in the way his hands moved over the controls, and a steeliness in the way his head sat on his thin neck.

They didn't make much conversation, but Ron gathered that the boy was a member of something called the Red Rockets, an organization with some inexplicable purpose.

It was only after the copter had landed on the roof of a half-decayed slum in the worst part of town, that Ron realized who the Red Rockets were. They were kids, all of them, banded together for mutual defense and in common antagonism toward the world. When he clambered out of the copter, his rescuer grinned and said:

"This is it, pal. This is where the gang meets."

"The Red Rockets?"

"Yeah. This is Shock's house. He's the leader."

They had to descend by stairs; there was no building elevator. When they reached the second floor, the boy put a finger to his lips, and rapped one-two, two-two on the apartment door.

A boy no older than Ron's new body opened it. His dark pinched face grew smaller and darker when he saw the stranger. He looked back into the room before letting them in.

The room was a study in decay. Someone had once wallpapered it in an optimistic pink pattern that was now sardonic in the surroundings. The furniture was rudimentary, and there were no working light fixtures. A battery lamp was sitting in the middle of a wooden table, and three youngsters were playing with a ragged deck of cards.

The tallest of them arose when the newcomers entered. He was the only one wearing a jacket; the others were in shirtsleeves. His hair was black, and unruly to the point of being ludicrous. His wide mouth twisted when he spoke.

"Who's this?" he said. "What's the idea?"

"He's okay," Ron's protector said. "He's an okay kid. I spotted him on a rooftop down on Park. A million cops after him. I dropped down in the copter and picked him up."

The tall boy studied Ron's face. "What's your name?"

"Ron."

"What were the cops chasin' you for?"

Ron hesitated. "Any of your business?"

The tall boy smiled. "Maybe not." He looked towards the others, and winked as if pleased. "Guess he's okay." He held his right hand out to Ron, while his left ducked into his jacket pocket. "My name's Shock, pal. And I'm the leader here. And just so's you don't forget it—"

Pain lanced through Ron's arm and struck the base of his skull. He tried to free himself from the tall boy's grip, but his fingers wouldn't part from the other's flesh. He dropped to his knees in agony, until the grip was broken.

He looked up, his face damp.

"That's your 'nitiation," the tall boy grinned. "Now you know what's what, Ronnie boy. So if you want to join the Rockets, you'll know where your orders come from."

Shock helped him to his feet. "Right, Ronnie boy?"

Ron shook his head, still bewildered.

"Good deal," Shock said. "Now let's finish that game. You play, kid?"

"No," Ron said. He staggered towards a wooden chair on the side of the room and dropped on it heavily. "No," he repeated, still trying to regain his breath.

Play the game....

His rescuer sat beside him. "Don't mind that guy," he whispered. "He does that to everybody. He got some kind of a power in his hands. But he's not a bad guy. Honest."

"Sure," Ron said weakly.

"We get a lot of kicks," the boy said eagerly. "You'll see. We have dogfights with the other gangs. With copters. We only got one, that ain't so much. But we're figurin' on gettin' some PF's next year, if we can collect enough dough in the treasury...."

"That'll be great," Ron said. Then he dropped his hand on the other's arm. "Listen—is there any chance of takin' a trip? In the copter?"

"Yeah, sure," the boy said warily. "Only you gotta ask for it in advance. I mean, it's Rocket property, and you gotta sign for it. And even then, if Shock wants to use it—well...."

"Why?" Ron said. "Why's that? Because he's the leader?"

"Sure," the boy said simply. "That's the reason."

Ron looked across the room at the card players.

"How do you get to be the leader?"

"I dunno. Shock's the leader 'cause he can lick anybody in the Rockets. That makes sense, don't it?"

"Yes. I suppose so." He chewed his lip. "Listen. Let's say *I* was leader. Could I use the copter then? Any time I wanted?"

"Sure. I mean, if you're the leader, who's gonna stop you?"

"Yes," Ron said. He stood up and walked to the table, watching the cards as they were slapped on the wood.

"Hey, Shock," he said.

The tall boy didn't look up. "What is it?"

"You cheat." A thrill ran through Ron's new body as he said it, and he muttered a small prayer that his guess about Shock's power was correct.

"I *what*?"

"I've been watching you play, and you cheat. You don't even cheat good. You cheat sloppy."

The tall boy stood up slowly, and the other chairs were scraped back in anticipation.

"Now that's something," he said. "That's really something! The kid's here ten minutes, and right away he wants to be buried." His face became grim. "Boy, we've had 'em wise before, pal. But never like this."

Ron planted himself in front of him.

"So?" he said.

Shock's face clouded. "Say, are you kidding? You really like trouble that bad?"

His right hand lashed out, while the left headed for his jacket pocket. But it wasn't the right that Ron avoided. Both of his short arms shot out towards the tall boy's left, and stopped the descent of the arm. Shock's right hand thudded against Ron's shoulder, the blow only stinging him.

"Hey!" Shock cried. "Hey, you—"

It was a triumph for Ron. He had been right about the electrical circuit woven through Shock's clothing, the circuit he couldn't complete without his left hand tripping the mechanism in his pocket. With the power off, Shock's weapon was useless. He was caught by surprise, and Ron's quick-moving hands tumbled him to the floor.

Before he had a chance to do anything else, Ron was upon him with an upraised chair. He closed his eyes before he swung. The sound of the crash might have sickened him in other circumstances; now it sounded good and satisfying.

Ron looked around the room, panting.

"I'm the leader now," he said. "Understand? I'm the leader!"

The looked at each other uncertainly.

"I'm taking the copter for a while," Ron said, backing towards the door. "Any arguments?"

Nobody answered.

"Swell. So long, pals."

Outside the door, he ran all the way back to the roof and was off before the gang could follow.

The trip took almost two hours. Even Ron's experienced guidance of the controls couldn't push the old copter past its limits, and he was keeping a worried eye on the fuel gauge. It was with a sigh of relief that he dropped the vehicle atop a public parking station in the downtown district, within walking distance of the Government Medical Center.

The sun was dropping fast, and the Washington streets were still filled with Sunday sightseers who found nothing odd in the sight of a solitary twelve-year-old. When he entered the enormous U-shaped edifice that housed a hundred and one government medical projects, he was thinking fast about a plausible story for the receptionist. The best he could do was:

"I'm looking for Dr. Wilfred Minton. He—he's my uncle."

"Dr. Minton?" She was young, and the efficient type. "I'm sorry, but Dr. Minton's been on special assignment for some time. It's not easy to locate him."

"Oh, I know about that," Ron said airily. "But I was supposed to see him today. You see, my mom—his sister that is—she was in a very bad accident...." He swallowed hard, wondering if he was being believed.

The woman frowned. "Well, if it's an emergency, I suppose I could check with central control. If it's really important."

"Oh, it's important, all right!" He said this with great conviction.

"Very well, then." She picked up her telephone, and there was much transferring from party to party. Finally, she lowered the receiver, saying: "He's in the east wing. It's Security territory, so I'll have to see about a pass."

It took another ten minutes for her to locate the authority she was seeking. A young man with crinkly hair and a grim expression came briskly to the desk, asked him a few questions, and then signed his name on a document. Ron put the paper into the pocket of his coveralls, and followed the man to a bank of private elevators.

The man waved him inside one, and he couldn't resist a wide-eyed question.

"Gosh, mister. Are you from the FBI?"

The man couldn't conceal a small pleased grin. "That's right, son. Only you keep it a secret."

"Sure," Ron said. When the door closed and the elevator ascended, he grinned too. Being twelve had its advantages sometimes.

He got off the elevator, and a uniformed guard checked his paper and led him into an anteroom.

"You wait here, son," he said, and left.

Ron waited five minutes. When nothing happened, he tried an adjoining door. It was open. He stepped inside the next room, and saw that it was a bare room with nothing but a row of filing cabinets and an abandoned swivel chair with a definite list to port.

He went to the files and peered at the designation cards.

They read:

PROJECT SCHOLAR.

He shrugged, and tried to open the top file. It was locked. He tried the others, with no better luck.

Then he heard the voices in the anteroom.

For some reason, he sensed danger. He knew he shouldn't be in the file room, that if he were found his visit to Dr. Minton might come to a sudden end. He couldn't take the chance. He tiptoed to the front door of the file room and turned the knob. He slipped out, and ran on his toes down the empty corridor.

Quickly, without thought of the consequence, Ron opened still another door and closed it behind him.

He looked at the shining brass fixtures and ultra modern appliances, and wondered what a kitchen was doing in a government medical building. Then, when he heard a sound in the adjoining room, he reasoned that he had stumbled into someone's living quarters.

He went to a brown mahogany door and pushed against it gently, until he widened the crack sufficiently to make out the figure walking up and down in the other room.

When the man crossed his line of vision, Ron's breath tumbled out in a gasp.

It was his own body. His thirty-year-old body, with its six-foot-two frame of big bones and long muscles, its sandy, close-cropped hair, its brooding eyes and full mouth. It was Ron Carver. It was himself as he had been before.

"Here's the little rascal," a voice said behind him.

The crinkly-haired man took his arm roughly.

"Okay, kid. Let's hear it."

"Hear what?" Ron said plaintively. "I wasn't doing anything!"

"Sure," the guard sneered. "He wasn't doin' a thing. Just snoopin' around, that's all."

The swinging door opened.

"What's going on here?"

Ron Carver looked at himself; at his own face, now strange and stony; at his own eyes, now bright and disinterested; at his own mouth, now a thin line of discontent. He heard his own voice, in a dangerous inflection he had never known before.

"Sorry, sir," the guard said, reddening. "Didn't know you were inside. Wouldn't have disturbed you—"

"How did he get here?"

"Gosh, sir, I really don't know. He says he was lookin' for Dr. Minton—"

"Minton," Ron Carver's voice said. "Yes, of course. He would be looking for Minton, wouldn't he?"

"Sir?"

"Never mind. Bring the boy into my quarters. Then get Dr. Minton up here at once."

"Yes, sir!"

They pushed the swinging door open and shoved Ron ahead of them. The room was an anomaly in this pristine government building, a warm room of deep-colored woods and thick carpeting. He was placed in a leather chair, his feet not touching the floor. The two men exited, and Ron Carver's body walked to an oaken desk and sat in the padded swivel chair behind the blotter.

"Well," he said. "This is something of a surprise for me."

"And how about me?" Ron said hoarsely.

The man laughed. "Yes, we are both surprised. Was it Robert Burns? Yes, of course. 'To see ourselves as others see us....'" He chuckled, and reached for a cigarette. "Filthy habit, this. Don't know how I picked it up. Possibly a deep-seated trait of yours, Mr. Carver. Odd how these things can be transferred."

The door opened again.

"Dr. Minton!" Ron leaped to his feet.

The doctor's face went white behind the gray beard and moustache.

"Then you've found him," he said softly, to neither of them in particular.

"No," Ron Carver's body answered. "I didn't find him, doctor. Rather, he found us. Isn't that right, Mr. Carver?"

"Yes!" Ron said. "And now I want to know the truth!"

"I, too, need answers," the Ron-body said stiffly. "I need answers at once, Dr. Minton. I would think this requires an explanation."

"I couldn't do it," the doctor whispered. "I couldn't do what you wanted, Scholar."

"Do what?" Ron said.

"All right, then," the Ron-body said coldly. "You failed once. But you're far too intelligent to make the same mistake twice. So you have your assignment, Dr. Minton. I will get you the help you need. But kill this—this remnant—"

He turned away in disgust, and picked up the telephone. He spoke under his breath for a few moments, and then hung up. "Dr. Luther will be here in just a moment. He'll arrange things with the laboratory. It will all be very painless and quick."

Ron said: "What are you talking about?" He looked wildly towards the old man, who had aged even further since entering the room. "Dr. Minton—"

The door opened. A brisk young man, carrying a small valise, appeared.

"All set downstairs," he said.

"Good," the Ron-body answered. "Then get it over with."

Ron struggled for a moment in the young man's grip, but he found it iron.

"Please, Ron." Doctor Minton's eyes were moist. "Don't make any trouble. Please...."

The laboratory was in the basement of the building, an antiseptic room with the acrid odor of chemicals. Dr. Luther prepared something in a hypodermic syringe, while Dr. Minton strapped his former patient onto a padded examining table.

"Doctor ..." Ron whispered.

"Hush, Ron. It's all right...."

"But what is all this? Who am I?"

The doctor frowned. "You're Ronald Carver. You're the same Ronald Carver you always were. But you have made an exchange of bodies. That is all."

"But why? How?"

"I don't really know. God help us. It was *his* project from start to finish—that thing upstairs."

"Who is he?"

"A phenomenon. A mutation. A freak. A genius. A god. I can't explain him. He was born twelve years ago, to normal parents in the middle west. He was a recognized prodigy at the age of six months, a mathematical wizard at one, a scientific genius at three.... You've heard of this kind of thing, Ron. Once a generation, something like this. And once a millenium—a horror like this one."

"I don't understand! What is Project Scholar?"

"He is. All by himself. The government has taken charge of his abilities, at least for the time being." He snorted. "He's already done things I wouldn't have believed possible in five thousand years of evolution. And yet he is still only twelve years old...."

"Only twelve?" Ron squirmed in the straps. "Doctor! This body—"

"Yes, Ron. It's his, of course. He grew angry with it; wanted to discard it, like everything else which doesn't fit his conception of the fitness of things. It was awkward—a giant's brain in a child's body. So he developed a solution—an operation, involving the total transference of electrical energy...."

The doctor's shaggy head bowed. "He needed human help for that. That's when I was brought in as assistant. And it was my function to select the perfect body as a temporary house for his ego...."

"Temporary?"

"When this body ages and grows feeble, there will be another. Our friend has outwitted Death itself."

The doctor looked up, his jaw firm.

"I was instructed to destroy his body when the transference was completed. I couldn't do it, Ron. I managed to spirit you away where you would be cared for. It was almost a year before you came to your senses after the operation. By that time, I didn't know what to do with you. My first thought was the Roverwood Home, where I am a director, where you would be lost among many, many boys' faces...."

"But why me, doctor? Why me?"

"I had to choose someone, Ron. It was merely a question of who...."

Dr. Luther entered, priming the needle.

"Ready?" he said.

"One moment." The doctor's hand covered Ron's mouth, and he felt the contours of a small round pill against his lips. He realized he was meant to swallow it, and he did.

"Ready now," Dr. Minton said.

Dr. Luther performed the injection.

"Good night, sweet prince," he said gently.

When Ron awoke, it was under a blanket of darkness and ice.

He blinked until his eyes became accustomed to the impoverished light that was glowing behind a glass-paned door.

He was on a block of some cold composition, in what must have been the Medical Center's morgue. He reacted with revulsion at the thought, and leaped off. Then he saw that his left hand was holding a sheet of paper. He carried it to the meager light source and read it quickly:

Ron—

Don't wait another moment. You'll find a suit of clothes in the closet left. Leave through back stairway marked N. There is money in suit. Use it to leave the city. Do not return if you value your safety and the life of

M.

He found the clothes as directed, a neatly-cut suit of boy's clothing, with a small wallet stuffed with bills amounting to three hundred dollars. He dressed rapidly, opened the door, and peered down the hall. It was empty as he ran silently towards the exit marked N.

Now he was doubly in debt to Dr. Minton. But he couldn't spare the doctor even now, for his life had been given a new direction and purpose.

He was going to kill the Scholar.

He walked rapidly through the dark streets towards the public parking lot where the helicopter had been stored. He took the lift to the roof, and walked up to it quickly.

"It's about time, pal."

It was Shock, his hair tousled over his hard, bright eyes. There was a gun in his hand.

"I've been waitin' an hour, you punk. Think you were gettin' off so easy?"

"Look, Shock—"

"You thought you were a clever boy, didn't you? Well, I got news for you—"

"Look, I don't want to be leader. I just needed a copter for a few hours."

"Yeah, sure. Only you forgot something. We put Finder equipment on this baby a long time ago, so we could keep tabs on it."

"You can *have* the copter—"

"I don't want just the copter, Ronnie boy. I want to square a few things with you."

"Look, Shock. I'll make a deal with you. I'll give you two hundred bucks for that gun."

The tall boy's face changed. "What?"

"You heard me. You hand over that gun, I'll give you two hundred dollars."

His eyes narrowed. "Then what? I suppose you'd shoot me and take off. Uh-uh, pal."

"You can check the gun downstairs, and sell me the key."

"Okay," Shock said slowly. "But if you're pullin' something—" He balled his hands menacingly.

They went down to the lower level together. Shock bought himself a public locker, and shoved the gun inside. Then he held up the key.

"Here it is, pal. Two hundred bucks worth."

Ron handed him the money. Shock whistled at the sight of the bills.

"Now," Ron said. "Would you like to make a hundred more?"

He looked at Ron with respect. "Okay. What's the pitch?"

"I want you to make a phone call for me."

"Yeah, sure." Shock looked bewildered. Then Ron explained.

They reached the guard in the East Wing of the Medical Center without much difficulty. Shock crouched over the receiver and said:

"This is Dr. Luther. Something's happened; you better connect me with *him*."

"Okay, hold on."

There was a wait. Then Ron Carver's own voice, in its eerie new inflection, was on the other end.

"What is it?"

"This is Luther. Something's happened down here. I think the boy got away."

"What? Where are you?"

"In the morgue, downstairs. I think you better come down yourself."

"How could it happen?" The Ron-voice was raging. "How?"

"I don't know. But you better meet me here in ten minutes—"

Ron jabbed Shock in the side, and the tall boy slammed the receiver back into place with a relieved sigh.

"I don't get it," he said. "Who was that guy?"

"Me," Ron said, with a grim smile. He handed Shock the money, and watched him depart, still looking baffled. Then he went to the locker and removed the gun, stuffing it inside his jacket. It bulked large against his narrow chest.

He raced through the streets back to the medical center, heading for Exit N and the morgue.

Ron was waiting, gun poised, behind the empty slab. A shadow covered the dim light behind the glass-plated door, and the Ron-body entered the silent room.

He saw his own hand reaching out to flick on the light switch. He saw his own face register dismay and annoyance at the quiet scene.

Then the Ron-body turned and was about to leave.

"Stay awhile," Ron said.

He stood up, revealing the weapon, holding it in both of his small hands for firm control of the trigger.

"Well," his voice said.

"Yes, well," Ron answered. "Very well, thanks. Only I won't speak for you, Scholar. Because I don't think you're well at all. I think you're out of your mind...."

The Ron-lips curled.

"Naturally. Genius is akin to madness. It's one of the deep-rooted convictions of the human ego. It reflects their suspicion, their distrust of the superintelligent ... I understand you, Mr. Carver."

"And I don't understand you! You're something new to me. Maybe you're better than us, maybe you're worse. I don't know, Scholar. But that's not why I'm going to kill you—"

"Oh?"

"No! You think I want to kill you for the sake of the world? Because you're a menace to homo sapiens? Because of your contempt for us ordinary mortals? Hell, no, Scholar! I'm too ordinary myself. I'm killing you for *me*, for Ron Carver! Because I'm sore! Just plain sore!"

He raised the gun.

For a moment, Ron didn't know what had happened. Something else blurred his vision, a fast-moving figure bulking up in front of his target. It was only when he heard the voice that he recognized the intruder as Dr. Minton, and he saw then that the doctor had rescued the Scholar from certain death.

"Stop, Ron—"

"Doctor! Get out of the way!"

"No, Ron. You don't know what you're doing—"

The old man was shielding the Ron-body with his own. Ron put the weapon down.

"But why?" he said.

"Because this is no answer! This is the assassin's way—" He turned to the Ron-body, and his voice was shaking. "Listen, Scholar. I want to arbitrate. Will you listen?"

"Do I have a choice?"

"Yes!" the doctor said fiercely. "Life or death! Will you listen to my terms?"

The Ron-body shrugged. "All right."

"Very well. Then I want you to spare Ron Carver. I want you to allow me to deliver him into the hands of friends, deliver him alive and safe. In return, I promise that your twelve-year-old body will leave this Earth virtually at once. I will send it to the colony on Mars, where it will stay until adulthood. Will you allow this?"

The Scholar's smile was thin. "And that is your only condition?"

"My only one!"

"Doctor—" Ron stepped towards him. "You can't leave things as they are—"

"Are you willing, Scholar? Will you let Ron Carver live his life in peace?"

The Ron-body stiffened.

"Yes," he snapped.

"Ron—" the doctor waved towards him. "Hand him your gun."

"What?"

"Give it to him! We've made a pact."

Ron hesitated, and then extended the butt towards the Scholar. He took it with a slight bow, weighed it in his palm, and then slipped the weapon into his pocket.

"You did wisely," the doctor said, with noticeable relief. "If you had turned that gun on us, Scholar, I would have killed you on the spot." He patted the metallic bulk beneath his own coat. "I came prepared, too...."

The copter rose serenely towards the heavenly vault. Ron's small body was feeling the effects of the day's strain. It collapsed against the leathery cushions, the short arms and legs limp and dangling.

The doctor patted his knee. "Another few moments," he said.

"Where are we going?"

"To the spaceport in Winnipeg. I have a friend there. He has two children of his own, both born in the Mars Colony. He'll be returning there within the week."

"And you want me to go with him?"

"Yes, Ron. I want you to grow up all over again, and then return to Earth. It won't be easy for you, but there will be advantages. Your life span has been lengthened. And right now, you know, you're something of a prodigy yourself." He chuckled dryly.

"And what happens here?" Ron said bitterly. "What kind of Earth will I find on my return?"

"An older Earth. Perhaps a wiser Earth...."

"No, doctor." Ron forced himself to a sitting position. "Not with the Scholar alive and thriving, growing stronger and more intelligent with every passing year. It'll be *his* Earth when I return...."

The doctor stared at the night sky before answering.

"No, Ron. He'll never live to see it. I knew that when I selected *your* body to house his mind...."

"What do you mean?"

"I chose you for a reason, Ron. A vital reason. When you came to my office on your return from Andromeda, I discovered something about you which made up my mind. An ailment without a name or a symptom, found only rarely in the bodies of a few space travelers. You had it, Ron, and in a year or two, it would have struck you down with the savagery and surprise of lightning.

"It was then that I agreed to the Scholar's plan to exchange bodies. Agreed to it on my own terms, with the body of Ron Carver...."

"Then I'll die!" Ron said.

"No, Ron. You will live. It's the Scholar who has made the bad bargain...."

In the distance, the lights of the Winnipeg spaceport blinked a welcome.

CPSIA information can be obtained
at www.ICGtesting.com
Printed in the USA
LVHW041914090222
710699LV00008B/247

9 789355 890115